Parsons, Alexandra
Fit for life

	DATE DUE	
MR 1 0 '12		
AUG 1 4 2013		
NOV 1 5 2013		

LIFE EDUCATION

Fit for Life

Written by
Alexandra Parsons

Illustrated by
John Shackell and Stuart Harrison

FRANKLIN WATTS
A DIVISION OF GROLIER PUBLISHING
NEW YORK · LONDON · HONG KONG · SYDNEY
DANBURY, CONNECTICUT

First American Edition
© 1996 by Franklin Watts
A Division of Grolier Publishing
Sherman Turnpike
Danbury, Connecticut
06816

10 9 8 7 6 5 4 3 2 1

Library of Congress Cataloging-in-Publication Data
Parsons, Alexandra
    Fit for life
       p. cm. — (Life education)
    Includes index.
    Summary: Provides information on healthy living,
eating, grooming habits, and fitness.
      ISBN 0-531-14372-4 (lib. bdg.)
      1. Children — Health and hygiene — Juvenile
literature. 2. Health — Juvenile literature. [1.
Health, 2. Physical fitness.]
    I. Title.   II. Series.
    RA777 P35 1995
    613.8'1'083 — dc20   95-20922
                                        CIP AC

Edited by: Janet De Saulles
Designed by: Sally Boothroyd
Commissioned photography by: Steve Shott
Illustrations by: John Shackell and Stuart Harrison

Acknowledgments:
Commissioned photography by Steve Shott: title page; contents page; 4; 5; 6; 9; 10; 12; 18(both); 19; 25.
Researched photographs: Sally & Richard Greenhill 11; Science Photo Library 13 (both); 14 (all); 20; 21; Zefa 24; 26.
Artwork: Cartoon illustrations of "alien" by Stuart Harrison. Cover and all other cartoon illustrations by John Shackell.

The publisher and Life Education International are indebted to Vince Hatton and Laurie Noffs for their invaluable help.

The publisher would like to extend special thanks to all the actors who appear in the *Life Education* books (Key Stage 2):

Jessamy Heath   Danny Mancini
Dishni Payagale Don   Peter Wood
Young-min Kim   Stephen Miles
Debbie Okangi   Daisy Doodles
Michael Wood   Joseph Wood
Mark Wall   Simon Wall
Andrew Wall   Christopher Wall
Vanessa Neita   Amber Neita-Crowley
Jun King   Ken King
Ben Clewley

"Each second we live is a new and unique moment of the universe, a moment that will never be again....And what do we teach our children? We teach them that two and two make four and that Paris is the capital of France.

When will we also teach them: do you know who you are? You are a marvel. You are unique. In all the years that have passed, there has never been another child like you. And look at your body – what a wonder it is! Your legs, your arms, your clever fingers, the way you move. You may become a Shakespeare, a Michelangelo, a Beethoven. You have the capacity for anything. Yes, you are a marvel. And when you grow up, can you then harm another who is, like you, a marvel? You must cherish one another. You must work – we must all work – to make this world worthy of its children."

Pablo Casals

Hi! I'm Zapp. Excuse the intrusion. Just popped over from Pluto to check you all out.

CONTENTS

YOU ARE WHAT YOU EAT (AND DRINK

Your body is your most important possession. You own it, and you have to take care of it. Bodies need exercise, they need to be kept clean, and they need the right kind of fuel to keep them going. The right kind of fuel a balanced mixture of foods, and not too much and not too little.

WHAT'S IN FOOD?
Basically, energy. You need energy to do anything and everything, even to sleep and watch television. Without energy, a body can't work, a heart won't beat, and lungs won't expand, nor keep you going as you run for the bus.

THREE FOOD GROUPS
Food is made up of three main groups: carbohydrates, proteins, and fats. Most foods are a mixture of these three things, but some have more of one group than the others. Foods also contain vital vitamins and minerals.

CARBOHYDRATES
Foods rich in carbohydrates are our chief sources of energy. Cereals, grains, fruits, and vegetables all contain carbohydrates, and athletes are often encouraged to eat a lot of these while they are training. Some carbohydrates are better than others. Sugary foods such as cakes and biscuits contain carbohydrates, and they do give you instant energy. But most lack food to build up your body, so you feel tired shortly afterward.

You do not use up much energy when you are relaxing.

HIGH

ENERGY METER

LOW

PROTEINS
These are the foods that are the building blocks of our bodies. Your body needs these to make new body tissues and to repair damaged cells. You need to eat quite a bit of protein every day just to keep adequate stores in your body. Protein foods include meat, fish, beans, nuts, eggs, milk, and cheese.

You burn up lots of energy when you run.

HIGH

ENERGY METER

LOW

How about this, Earthlings! There's enough iron in a healthy human body to make a one-inch nail, and enough lime to whitewash a small shed.

FATS

Foods made mainly of fat help your body to store energy in the form of fat cells under your skin. You need a layer of fat as a reserve tank of energy, but you don't need too much. If a person is overweight, it usually means he or she has more than enough fat stored up and doesn't need to eat any more of it for a while. Foods high in fat include butter, cooking oil, ice cream, and cream.

MINERALS AND VITAMINS

These vital extras are found in a wide range of foods throughout all the food groups. Vitamins help your body to get the maximum amount of goodness from its food. Minerals are traces of salts and natural metals (such as iron) that nerves and muscles need to keep going. Bones and teeth need minerals too, both to grow and, in the case of bones, to repair themselves.

A DIET FOR HEALTH

To keep healthy, you should eat plenty of good carbohydrates, a medium amount of protein, and a small amount of fats.

NEXT FOOD GROUP PLEASE

NEXT FOOD GROUP PLEASE

T he good news is that eating healthy foods is a delicious experience. And because eating healthy food makes you feel good, you will have plenty of energy to do all the things you want to do. A healthy diet gives your disease-fighting system — the immune system — a real boost.

BREAKFAST MENU
A bowl of cereal with
low-fat milk
A piece of fresh fruit
or
A slice of whole wheat toast
with peanut butter and a
little jelly
A fruit yogurt
or
French toast
A glass of fresh fruit juice

HEALTHY DIET PYRAMID

A simple guide to healthy eating is to enjoy a good amount of cereals, bread, vegetables, and fruit; a moderate amount of meat, fish, eggs, nuts, milk, and cheese or yogurt; and just a little sugar, butter, and oil.

BREAKFAST

This is a very important meal. Make sure you get up early enough to enjoy it.

To make French Toast

You need 1 slice of bread, 1 egg, a little butter, a nonstick frying pan.

1 Beat the egg and pour the egg mixture onto a plate.

2 Dip the bread into the egg, pressing it down so the egg soaks through.

3 Heat up the butter in the pan. When it starts to sizzle, put the bread in the pan and cook it on both sides until the egg has set and the bread has turned a golden yellow.

Serve with a little salt, or sugar, or maple syrup — but not all three at once.

Did you know that the sandwich was invented by the Earl of Sandwich, an eighteenth century gambler so addicted to the card table that he didn't have time for regular meals? "Just bring me a slice of ham between two pieces of bread," he commanded the waiter, and the rest is history.

. . . . . CHOOSING WISELY . . . . .

Learn to be tempted by foods that make you feel good. When you are choosing what to eat with what, try not to choose all your foods from the same category. For instance, if you want a hamburger and chips for lunch, have an apple for dessert. If you choose salad and a baked potato, you could enjoy a chocolate bar or an ice cream afterward. If you accidentally pig out on a really greasy meal, make sure that the next day you eat some extra fruits and vegetables to balance things out.

MAKE A MENU

Make up a healthy lunch from the items below, choosing three items (or four if you're extra hungry).

Salad with cheese
  or ham
Hamburger
Vegetable curry
Fried fish

Portion of fries
Baked potato
Rice
Slice of bread

Fresh fruit
Peas
Cauliflower with
  cheese
Raw carrots
  and dips

Ice cream
Pudding or custar
Low-fat yogurt
Chocolate bar
Stewed fruit

COOKING FOR HEALTH

The way foods are cooked makes a difference. Raw vegetables are very good for you. Even when vegetables are cooked they should not be boiled for too long, because that takes all the nutrients out of them, and leaves them in the cooking water.

Even the healthiest foods become fatty if they are cooked with too much oil. On the right of this page is a way of making nongreasy, delicious potato chips to have with your supper.

Get into the habit of taking a healthy packed lunch to school with you.

To Make Potato Chips

You need 1 large potato, 2 teaspoons vegetable oil, a little sweet paprika, a cookie sheet.

1 Turn the oven on to 400° F (200° C or Gas Mark 6). Scrub the potato but don't peel it.

2 Ask an adult to help you cut the potato into thin rings.

3 Brush half the vegetable oil onto the cookie sheet. Arrange the potato slices in one layer on the sheet, and brush them with the remaining oil.

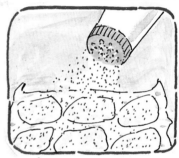

4 Sprinkle with the paprika and bake for 20 minutes. Reduce the heat to 300° F (150° C or Gas Mark 2) and bake for another 30 minutes, or until the chips are crisp and brown.

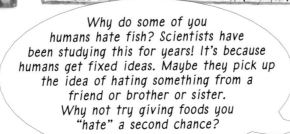

Why do some of you humans hate fish? Scientists have been studying this for years! It's because humans get fixed ideas. Maybe they pick up the idea of hating something from a friend or brother or sister. Why not try giving foods you "hate" a second chance?

The bad news is that some ways of eating can make you sick, overweight, lazy, and moody. You can understand why if you think of your body as an amazing machine that runs at its best on top-grade, five-star superfuel. It's not going to give you much of a performance if you fill it with nothing but sludgy gunk is it? (The occasional indulgence is okay!)

NOW AND AGAIN FOODS

Foods that are high in sugars, salts, and fats and low in body-building protein and long-term energy boosters are not the kind of foods you want to live on. If you eat too much fat, your fat deposits will increase, but you will not have any energy. If you eat too much sugar, you will only get a quick spurt of energy and will soon feel tired. Some fatty, sugary foods are delicious and are okay for the occasional treat or snack, but only once in a while.

Which fuel would you choose?

QUESTION:

How do you think you would feel after a week of eating only from foods on this list?
French fries, potato chips,
bag of candy, chocolate,
ice cream, cakes,
soda, jello.

FOOD AND FEELING GOOD ABOUT YOURSELF

A lot of people find eating very comforting, and sometimes they eat too much, maybe because they feel they are not getting love and comfort from friends and family. Other people (usually teenage girls) often think that food is their enemy and starve themselves, sometimes to death. These are called eating disorders. They are emotional problems that need special help.

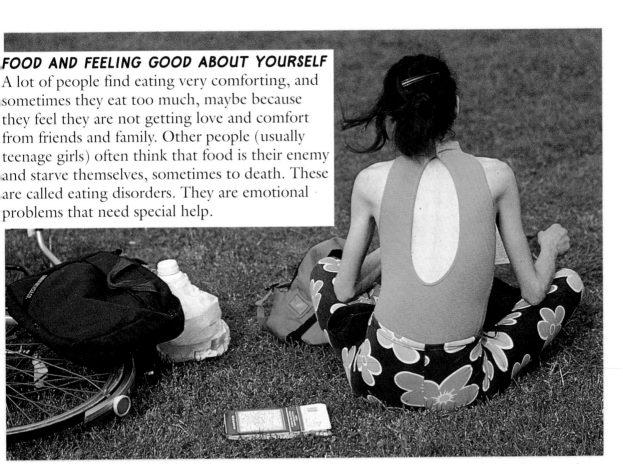

This girl doesn't eat enough. She is suffering from anorexia nervosa, an illness that makes people feel they need to be thinner, even if they are already underweight. People who have this illness find it very difficult, even frightening, to admit that they are not well and that they need help.

You remember kids, people come in all sorts of shapes and sizes – you cannot change the basic shape you were born with.

ANSWER: *Pretty sick.*

. . . . DRINK THIS! . . . . . .

What is the best possible drink in the world? What is the drink your body craves? Water. Clear, fresh water. Sixty-five percent of our body weight is water and it needs plenty of fluids. Water does not contain any nutrients, but it usually has traces of minerals. It is second only to air in things the body needs.

PROTEIN AND ENERGY DRINKS

Milk is good for you because it contains protein (those building blocks the body needs). Fruit juices will give you an energy boost because they contain natural sugars. Milk and fruit juices also contain vitamins and minerals. Most drinks you can buy in cans or bottles contain quite a lot of sugar. Sports drinks usually contain glucose, a simple form of sugar easily absorbed by the body, and they contain minerals. The minerals are added because you sweat some of these out of your body when you exercise.

SO WHAT ABOUT ALCOHOL?

For most adults, drinking in moderation (one or two glasses once in a while) may be okay. For children it is not okay at all. Children's livers and brains are still busy developing, and it's just too much to ask them to cope with alcohol.

NO ALCOHOL PLEASE, I'M STILL GROWING!

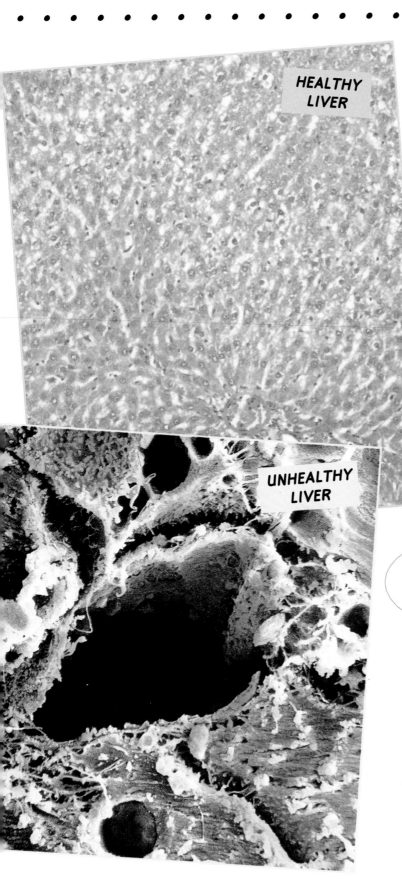

HEALTHY LIVER

UNHEALTHY LIVER

HOW ALCOHOL AFFECTS THE LIVER

Alcohol does not need to be digested; it is absorbed right into the bloodstream through the walls of the stomach and small intestine. It circulates around the body and goes straight up to the brain, where it causes disorientation.

Alcohol also goes to the liver where it damages liver cells. It can only be turned into sugar at the rate of about one glassful an hour. If there is any more than that in the bloodstream, the alcohol keeps circulating around until the liver can process more. Consistently overloaded livers become damaged and scarred and eventually just stop working.

Turn the page, if you dare, and find out what too much alcohol can do to your brain, heart, and stomach.

... THE DAMAGE CONTINUES ...

T he liver is not the only organ that can be harmed by too much alcohol. The brain, stomach and heart can also be badly damaged.

THE BRAIN
People who drink too much are destroying their brain cells at an alarming rate. Alcohol stops the brain working properly. Drunk people often can't walk straight because their brains don't send the right messages to the right muscles. They often say very stupid things or make no sense at all because the brain has lost control of the centers of speech and thought. People who drink too much alcohol also make bad decisions and may harm themselves and others.

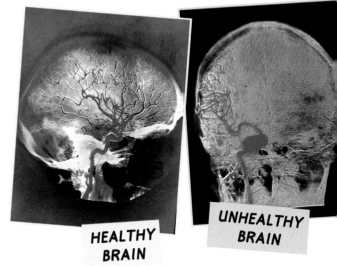

HEALTHY BRAIN

UNHEALTHY BRAIN

THE STOMACH
Alcohol irritates the lining of the stomach. Too much drink may cause ulcers, or sores in the stomach wall, as well as vomiting or diarrhea or both.

THE HEART
The heart of a heavy drinker is often swollen because alcohol damages the heart muscle. It also tends to make people overweight, as alcohol is fattening.

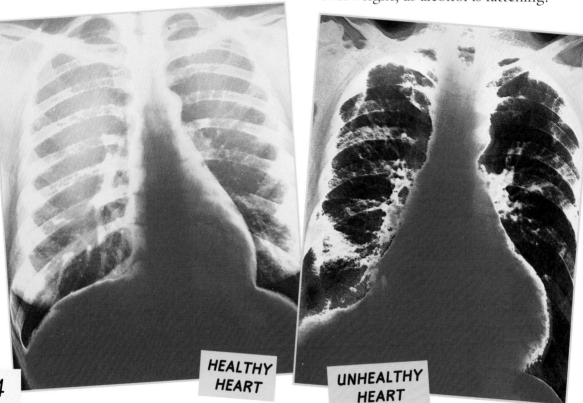

HEALTHY HEART

UNHEALTHY HEART

ONE DRINK TOO MANY . . .

The problems start when people drink too much, and that is very easily done. When one glass feels good, it's easy to think that six are going to feel six times as good. But that's not the case at all. People who have overloaded with alcohol are likely to stumble, be sick, say something stupid, pick a fight with a friend, and wake up feeling terrible.

BRAIN CELL TO MARVIN: PUT RIGHT HAND OUT.

BRAIN CELL TO MARVIN: SAY HELLO TO MRS. OSGOOD.

Hello, Mrs. Osgood!

A FEW DRINKS LATER . . .

PUT GLASS ON TABLE!

SAY GOODBYE TO MRS. OSGOOD!

No Good Mrs. Bye Bye...

THE MESSAGES JUST AREN'T GETTING THROUGH, CEDRIC. WE MIGHT AS WELL PULL DOWN THE SHADES AND GET SOME SLEEP.

Bang!

Being drunk isn't funny: it's annoying and it can be dangerous.

What a rude boy!

15

17

. . . . GET FIT AND FLEXIBLE . . . .

All the muscles in your body need exercise, including your heart and the muscles around your lungs. Strong heart and lungs deliver lots of oxygen to every cell in the body. A body with a good oxygen supply is a lively, energetic body with a hard-working immune system that is less likely to get sick. A mind with a good oxygen supply is a sharp mind.

AEROBICS

There is no way of actually exercising your heart and breathing muscles directly, so to give your hearts and breathing muscles a workout you have to do exercises that make them work overtime. Any form of exercise that makes your heart beat faster and makes you breathe faster is called aerobic exercise. Aerobic is a word made up from two Greek words meaning *life* and *air*. It takes about 2 minutes of continuous exercise to get your heart and lungs going.

HOW TO GET FIT

Providing you are already healthy, you will be fit if you do aerobic exercise continuously for 20 minutes 3 times a week. These are some aerobic activities: running, skipping, cycling, swimming, rowing.

BEFORE EXERCISE

You must prepare the body by warming up and stretching, so that muscles don't get injured. Hold stretches for 8 – 10 seconds, relax, and then repeat. Do not bounce.

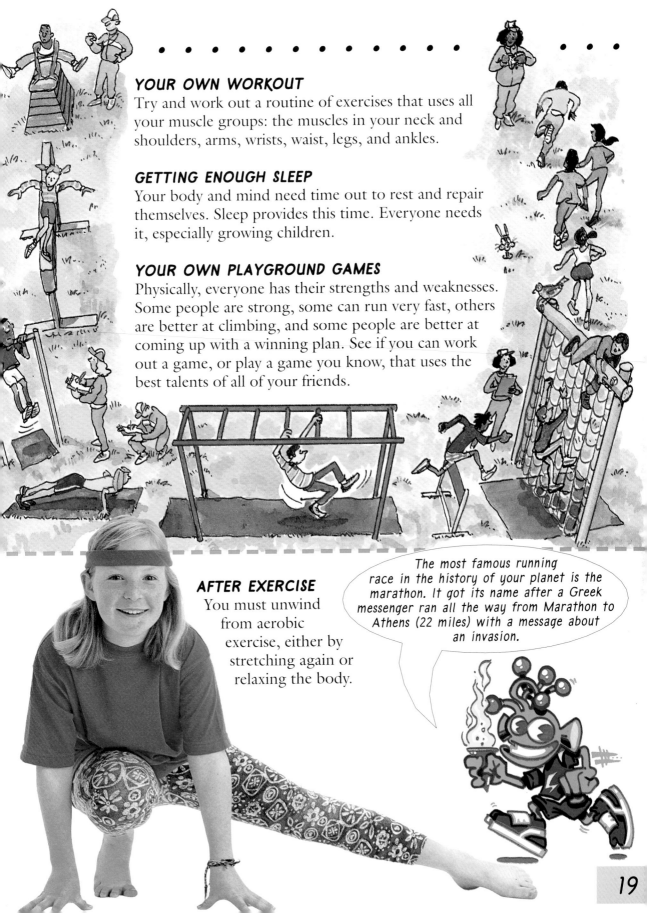

YOUR OWN WORKOUT

Try and work out a routine of exercises that uses all your muscle groups: the muscles in your neck and shoulders, arms, wrists, waist, legs, and ankles.

GETTING ENOUGH SLEEP

Your body and mind need time out to rest and repair themselves. Sleep provides this time. Everyone needs it, especially growing children.

YOUR OWN PLAYGROUND GAMES

Physically, everyone has their strengths and weaknesses. Some people are strong, some can run very fast, others are better at climbing, and some people are better at coming up with a winning plan. See if you can work out a game, or play a game you know, that uses the best talents of all of your friends.

AFTER EXERCISE

You must unwind from aerobic exercise, either by stretching again or relaxing the body.

The most famous running race in the history of your planet is the marathon. It got its name after a Greek messenger ran all the way from Marathon to Athens (22 miles) with a message about an invasion.

19

. . . LOOK AFTER YOUR LUNGS . .

In the same way that what you eat and drink affects your body, what you breathe in affects it too. Just think how you cough and sputter if you catch a lungful of exhaust fumes. People who live near main roads, factories that produce a lot of smoke, or fields that get sprayed with pesticides may get lung diseases like asthma and bronchitis. People who are lucky enough to breathe clean air tend to have healthier lungs.

FROM LUNG TO BLOOD SUPPLY

Because the lungs deliver oxygen directly into the blood, any fumes that get into the lungs also get into the blood. This is why breathing bad air makes people sick. Breathing in certain poison gases or fumes can kill in an instant.

A LUNGFUL OF POISON GAS

There are few worse things than a lungful of cigarette smoke. Cigarette smoke contains gases that harm the nose and throat's defense mechanisms for protecting the lungs. It also contains tar that sticks to lung cells and affects their working; and nicotine, a drug that zips straight to the nervous system and gives it a little kick. But not for long.

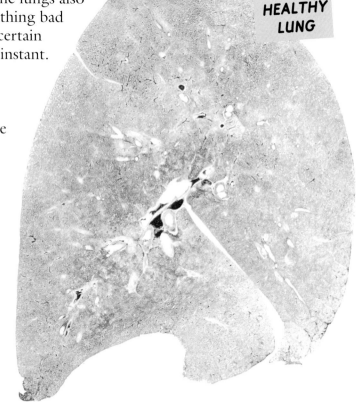

HEALTHY LUNG

WHAT'S THE EXCITEMENT?

Nicotine is an addictive drug that you keep needing more and more of to have any effect. That means it makes your body crave it. It is very easy to get addicted to smoking and very hard to give it up. In the end people may find themselves going through two or more packs a day just to feel "normal."

They don't tell you any of this in those cigarette advertisements do they? I wonder why not?

SO WHAT'S THE DAMAGE?

Immense. Nicotine isn't the only problem here, although being addicted to anything is harmful, and there seems very little point in being addicted to something expensive that in the end just makes you feel normal. The tars and gases are an even bigger problem. They destroy lung tissue, as well as enter the bloodstream and damage that too. Smokers not only have damaged lungs, they very often have enlarged hearts, swollen veins, bad circulation, bad skin, smelly breath, wrinkled faces, stained fingers and teeth. And many will die of illnesses caused by smoking.

SO WHY DO PEOPLE SMOKE?

That is a very difficult question to answer. Maybe nobody told them how harmful it was. Maybe they didn't listen. Maybe they thought they knew best. Maybe they were talked into starting by people who they thought were their friends.

UNHEALTHY LUNG

MAKING THE BEST OF YOURSELF

Your skin is the largest organ of your body. Apart from protecting your body, it helps regulate your body temperature; it sends messages to your brain about what you are touching and feeling; it produces hair and nails in all the right places; and it helps to fight off infection. Your skin reflects your general state of health. Clear skin with a healthy glow looks very attractive.

It is important to protect your skin from sunburn. Sun block can be fun to wear.

KEEP IT CLEAN

Skin does its work better if it is kept clean. You should wash off perspiration. Sweat tends to smell and your skin might remain damp (feet especially). You should wash off dirt in case you accidentally cut or scratch yourself and dirt gets into the skin. You should always wash your hands after you have been to the bathroom to prevent bacteria from spreading around.

Your blemishes might just be because you are growing up. Lots of young people get zits from time to time. Just keep clean — and don't pick at them!

All you need to keep clean.

SWEAT GLANDS

Skin is made up of several layers. In the layer just below the surface, you have three million sweat glands. Their job is to keep you cool. Beads of sweat (which are actually body wastes — mainly water and salts) pop out of the pores of your skin, and as they evaporate in the air, your skin cools down. You get rid of these evaporated body wastes by washing!

Ouch! Roasting in the sun can cause a lot of damage.

SUNTANS

Being out in the sunlight stimulates special pigment cells in your skin that turn you brown, to help protect your skin from burning. But it can do only so much. Too much sunshine dries up the skin and can cause skin cancer. So always remember to use plenty of high-protection suntan lotion. It's better to be pale than wrinkled, and much better than getting skin cancer! Use a moisturizing cream if your skin feels at all dry.

HAIR AND NAILS

Clean shiny hair looks better than greasy rats' tails. Nails should be kept clean and well cut. All kinds of interesting germs can get stuck under nails, which may find their way into the body through the nail bed.

TEETH

Healthy, strong teeth look a lot better than unhealthy ones! If you brush teeth properly twice a day you should be able to control the buildup of sticky, yellow plaque that attacks the teeth and causes decay.

. . . . WHAT ARE DRUGS? . . . . .

When you get sick, your body becomes a raging battle ground between your immune system, which fights off disease, and bacteria or viruses. Bacteria produce poisons, and viruses get inside cells in our bodies and change the way the cells work.

All drugs change the way the body works. Medicinal drugs, used properly, help us to get better.

DOCTORS AND MEDICINE

A doctor's job is to find the right way to help your body overcome the problems it is having. Medicines and drugs can make a sick body better. Drugs enter the bloodstream through the stomach, the lungs, or through injection. Drugs are chemicals that change the way the body works. Carefully prescribed drugs can often make sick people better.

THREE TIMES A DAY AFTER MEALS

Some very useful medicines, such as aspirin or cough medicine, can be bought from a drug store without a prescription. But they must still be used according to the directions. This is because *anything* that changes the way the body works has to be used *very* carefully, and *very* precisely. Too much aspirin, for instance, can cause the stomach to bleed.

DRUGS ARE POWERFUL

Some people have to take certain drugs for their lifetime. Some diabetics, for instance, whose bodies lack the ability to break down sugars, need to take insulin every day. In nondiabetics, insulin is made in sufficient amounts, and regulated by the body itself. If a nondiabetic started taking insulin, the body would activate all kinds of emergency reactions. *Never* take medicines or drugs prescribed for someone else. A DRUG YOU DON'T NEED IS A POISON.

BRAIN CELL REGENERATOR

EXTRA OXYGEN SUPPLY

EAR PLUGS TO KEEP OUT GOOD ADVICE

UNLIMITED CASH FOR FINANCING EXPENSIVE DRUG HABIT

SPARE LUNGS

SPARE LIVER

OVERDOSE WARNING METER

CHEMICAL FILTERING PLANT

ROCKET BOOTS FOR ESCAPING POLICE DRUG RAIDS

The human body is not made to cope with drug abuse. Drugs affect the delicate balance within the body and often kill off cells and wear out organs that are made to work harder as they try to deal with the drugs. These cells and organs can never be naturally replaced.

USE AND ABUSE

Some drugs that act on the nervous system are taken by people who don't need to take them for medical reasons. They take them to *feel* different. Using drugs for the wrong reasons, or to excess, is drug abuse. The drugs mess up the complicated workings of the body, especially of the immune system. A damaged immune system means a body that cannot recover from illness. The body cannot cope with repeated use of poisons and chemicals. It may react by shutting parts of itself down, or by becoming dependent on even larger doses of the drug in question, or possibly both. This state is called addiction. Once addicted, it is almost impossible to quit and start afresh. There are better ways to feel good.

What's the best feeling in the whole universe? Well I've checked out just about everything, everywhere, and I'll tell you what I've learned. The best feeling is feeling good about being yourself!

27

REMIND ME, AM I HAVING FUN?

Which would you choose?

Drug use, and that includes smoking cigarettes, sniffing solvents, and drinking too much alcohol, can make children or adults very sick.

People who take drugs hang around with people who encourage them to keep abusing. Drug abusers have little time for real friends.

28

Drugs are expensive.

There are many decisions that we have to make as we grow up. Sometimes these decisions can be confusing. If you find yourself faced with a confusing decision there are always people who can help you to discuss the choices: your mom or dad, or teacher for starters! The thing to remember is that your life is yours. You are in charge. You can choose which pathway you want to walk down.

Well, I know what choices I'd make if I were a human.

LETTER FROM LIFE EDUCATION

Dear Friends:

The first Life Education Center was opened in Sydney, Australia, in 1979. Founded by the Rev. Ted Noffs, the Life Education program came about as a result of his many years of work with drug addicts and their families.

Ted Noffs realized that preventive education, beginning with children from the earliest possible age all the way into their teenage years, was the only long-term solution to drug abuse and other related problems, including violence and AIDS.

Life Education pioneered the use of technology in a futuristic "Classroom of the 21st Century," designed to show in an exciting way the beauty of life on planet Earth and how drugs including nicotine and alcohol can destroy the delicate balance of human life itself. In every Life Education classroom, there are electronic displays that show the major body systems including the respiratory, nervous, digestive, and immune systems. There is a talking brain and wondrous star ceiling. And there is Harold the Giraffe who appears in many of the programs and is Life Education's official mascot. Programs start in preschool and go all the way through high school.

There are parents' programs and violence prevention classes. Life Education has also begun to create interactive software for home and school computers as well as having its own home page on the Internet, the global information superhighway (the address is http://www.lec.org/).

There are Life Education Centers operating in seven countries (Thailand, the United States, the United Kingdom, New Zealand, Australia, Hong Kong, and New Guinea).

This series of books will allow the wonder and magic of Life Education to reach many more young people with the simple message that each human being is special and unique and that in all of the past, present, and future history there will never be another person exactly the same as you.

If you would like to learn more about Life Education International, contact us at one of the addresses listed below or, if you have a computer with a modem, you can write to Harold the Giraffe at Harold@lec.org and you'll find out that a giraffe can send E-mail!

Let's learn to live.

All of us at the Life Education Center.

Life Education, USA
149 Addison Ave
Elmhurst, Illinois
60126
Tel: 708-530-8999
Fax: 708-530-7241

Life Education, UK
20 Long Lane
London
EC1A 9HL
United Kingdom
Tel: 0171-600-6969
Fax: 0171-600-6979

Life Education,
Australia
29 Hughes Street
Potts Point
NSW 2011
Australia
Tel: 0061-2-358-2466
Fax: 0061-2-357-2569

Life Education,
New Zealand
126 The Terrace
PO Box 10-769
Wellington
New Zealand
Tel: 0064-4-472-9620
Fax: 0064-4-472-9609

GLOSSARY

Aerobic exercises These increase the amount of oxygen you breathe in, strengthening your heart and lungs.

Bacteria Tiny living organisms that can make you ill if they enter your body.

Carbohydrates These give you energy. Cereals, fruits, and vegetables contain carbohydrates.

Cells Your body is made up of millions of these: your brain is made up of brain cells, your liver of liver cells, and so on.

Fats Fats help to store energy in fat cells under your skin. Butter, margarine, cream, and cooking oil contain fats.

Glucose A simple form of sugar.

Immune system This helps protect you against diseases.

Minerals Minerals are found in tiny amounts in many foods. They keep your body working well.

Nicotine A poisonous and addictive substance found in cigarettes.

Nutrients The goodness in food.

Perspiration Another name for sweat.

Pores Tiny openings in your skin that allow it to breathe.

Proteins Protein is essential for building up your body and developing strong muscles. Meat, fish, eggs, cheese, milk, beans, and nuts contain proteins.

Ulcer An open sore. It can develop inside your body, for example on the lining of your stomach.

Virus Tiny living organisms that can make you ill by changing the way your cells work.

Vitamins Different vitamins are found in different foods. They help your body take the goodness from the food you give it.

FURTHER INFORMATION

These organizations can help you with your questions:

Al-Anon Family Group Headquarters
P.O. Box 862
Midtown Station
New York, NY 10018
Telephone: 212-302-7240
Toll-free: 800-356-9996
Fax: 212-869-3757

American Anorexia/Bulimia Association
418 E. 76th Street
New York, NY 10021
Telephone: 212-734-1114
Fax: 212-879-8249

American Lung Association
1740 Broadway
New York, NY 10019
Telephone: 212-315-8700
Fax: 212-265-5642

TARGET
Helping Students Cope with Tobacco, Alcohol, and Other Drugs
11724 NW Plaza Circle
P.O. Box 20626
Kansas City, MO 64195
Telephone: 816-464-5400
Toll-free: 800-366-6667
Fax: 816-464-5571

INDEX